Classic
Put-downs

Classic Put-downs

Witty replies and comic remarks

SIRIUS

SIRIUS

This edition published in 2019 by Sirius Publishing, a division of
Arcturus Publishing Limited,
26/27 Bickels Yard, 151–153 Bermondsey Street,
London SE1 3HA

ISBN: 978-1-78828-588-9
AD006401NT

Printed in China

Contents

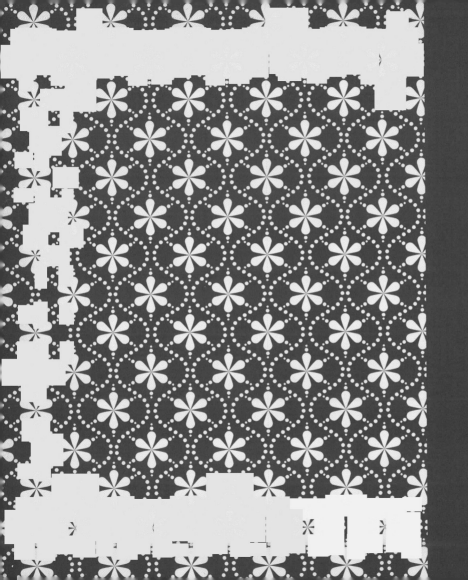

Classic
Put-downs

Political
Brickbats

In politics if you want anything said, ask a man. If you want anything done, ask a woman.

Margaret Thatcher, British Prime Minister

Attila the Hen.

Clement Freud, British politician, about Margaret Thatcher

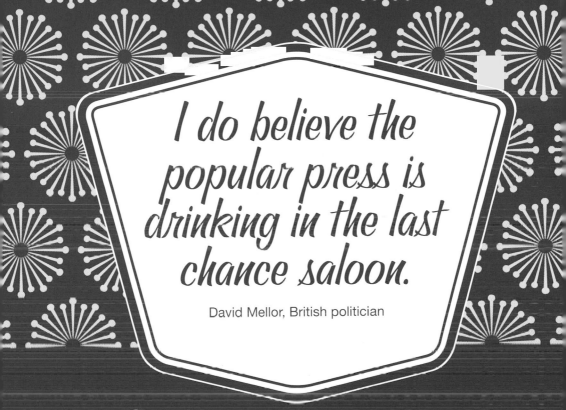

I do believe the popular press is drinking in the last chance saloon.

David Mellor, British politician

Politics have no relation to morals.

Niccolo Machiavelli, Italian political theorist

Tony Blair is so weak and vulnerable that Madonna is thinking of adopting him.

Rory Bremner, British satirist

A working man voting for Ronald Reagan is like a chicken voting for Colonel Sanders.

Paul Sarbanes, US Senator

Reagan won because he ran against Jimmy Carter. If he'd run unopposed he would have lost.

Mort Sahl, US comedian

Say what you will about Trump, he is not stupid. He is a smart man with a deep understanding of what stupid people want.

Andy Borowitz

An appeaser is one who feeds a crocodile, hoping it will eat him last.

Winston Churchill, British Prime Minister

One of the penalties for refusing to participate in politics is that you end up being governed by your inferiors.

Plato, Greek philosopher

I have never seen such a slippery candidate.

Nat Hentof, US journalist, on Bill Clinton, US President

Sex with Nicholas was like having a very large wardrobe with a very small key falling on top of you.

Ex-lover of British politician, Nicholas 'Fatty' Soames

It is remarkable how easily children and grown-ups adapt to living in a dictatorship organised by lunatics.

A. N. Wilson, British writer

When I am right, I get angry. Churchill gets angry when he is wrong. We are angry at each other much of the time

French President Charles de Gaulle on British Prime Minister Winston Churchill

...that seems only fair, we had them last time!

Winston Churchill, British Prime Minister, before WWII, when Nazi Germany declared that the Italians would be on Germany's side

The best argument against democracy is a five-minute conversation with the average voter.

Winston Churchill, British Prime Minister

I married beneath me. All women do.

Lady Astor, first woman to sit as an MP in the British House of Commons

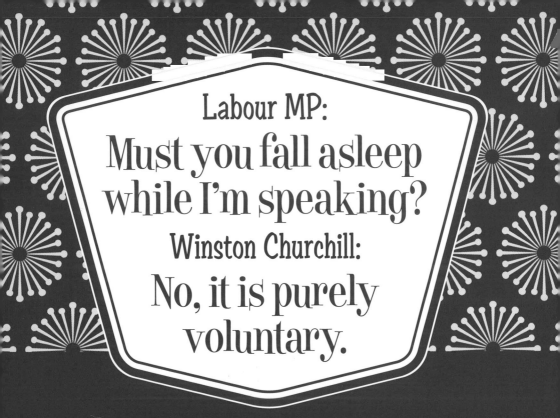

Labour MP:

Must you fall asleep while I'm speaking?

Winston Churchill:

No, it is purely voluntary.

He says he works out because it clears his mind. Sometimes just a little too much.

Jay Leno, US comedian and chat show host, on George W Bush

To err is Truman.

A catchphrase during the Truman presidency in 1946

Bessie Braddock, British MP, to Winston Churchill:

Mr Churchill, you are drunk.

Churchill:

Bessie, you are ugly. But I'll be sober in the morning.

You've no idea what it costs to keep the old man in poverty.

Lord Louis Mountbatten on Mahatma Gandhi

Political Brickbats

Senator, you're no Jack Kennedy.

Lloyd Bentsen, US Senator, to Dan Quayle during the 1988 United States vice-presidential debate

That's got every fire hydrant in America worried.

Bill Clinton, US President, on hearing that Dan Quayle had promised to be 'like a pitbull' in their battle for the US presidency

US President William Howard Taft:

There is so much noise, I can hardly hear myself talk.

Heckler:

That's all right, you're not missing anything.

Never murder a man when he's busy committing suicide.

Woodrow Wilson, US President

Political Brickbats

He can compress the most words into the smallest idea of any man I know.

Abraham Lincoln, US President
on a political rival

Does the Honourable Lady remember that she was an egg herself once: and very many members of all sides of this House regret that it was ever fertilized?

Sir Nicholas Fairbairn, British politician, attacking
junior Health Minister Edwina Currie over a scare about
salmonella in eggs

20

You show the bourgeoisie your behind.
We, on the contrary, look them in the face.

Georgi Plekhanov, Russian Social Democrat, to Vladimir Ilyich Lenin

A foreign diplomat on finding Abraham Lincoln polishing his boots:
Mr President! You black your own boots?

Lincoln:
Yes. Whose boots do you black?

If I had another face, do you think I would wear this one?

Abraham Lincoln, US President,
on being called two-faced

Political Brickbats

Sumner's mind had reached calm water which receives and reflects images without absorbing them; it contained nothing but itself.

Henry Adams, US journalist, on politician Charles Sumner

Fritz Hollings, US Senator, when challenged to take a drug test during a TV debate with Republican candidate Henry McMaster:

I'll take a drug test if you'll take an IQ test.

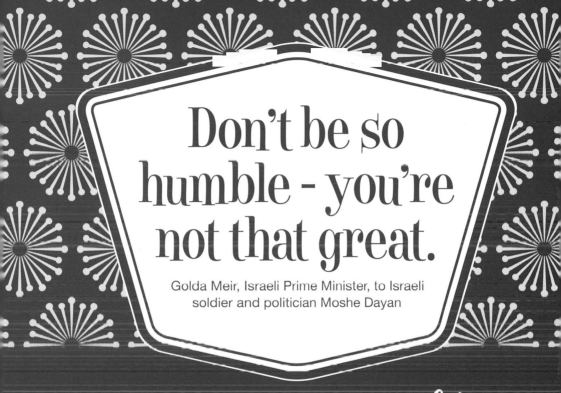

Don't be so humble - you're not that great.

Golda Meir, Israeli Prime Minister, to Israeli soldier and politician Moshe Dayan

Behind every successful man is a surprised woman.

Mary Pearson, wife of Lester Pearson, Canadian Prime Minister

Douglas can never be President, Sir. His legs are too short and his coat, like a cow's tail, hangs too near the ground, Sir.

Thomas Hart Benton, US Senator, on presidential candidate Stephen A. Douglas

As thin as the homeopathic soup that was made by boiling the shadow of a pigeon starved to death.

US President Abraham Lincoln ridiculing a rival's proposal

He is, like almost all the eminent men of this country, only half-educated. His morals, public and private, are loose.

John Quincy Adams, US President, on US Senator Henry Clay

Brilliant to the top of his army boots.

Lloyd George, British Prime Minister, on field marshal Douglas Haig

Political Brickbats

Reagan's in the news again. He's at his ranch chopping wood - he's building the log cabin he was born in.

Johnny Carson, US comedian and TV host

If ever he went to school without any boots it was because he was too big for them.

Ivor Bulmer-Thomas, British journalist and MP, mocking Labour Prime Minister Harold Wilson's claim to a deprived childhood

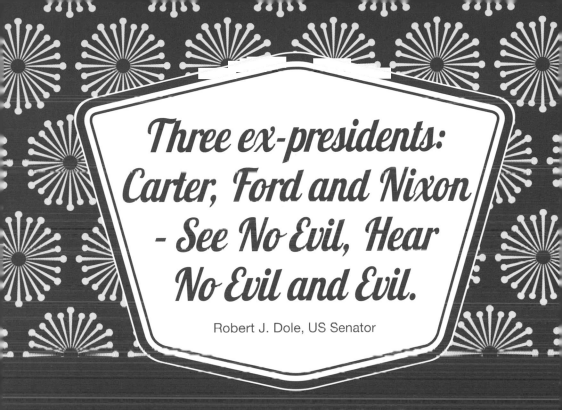

Three ex-presidents:
Carter, Ford and Nixon
- See No Evil, Hear
No Evil and Evil.

Robert J. Dole, US Senator

He knows nothing and thinks he
knows everything. That points clearly to a
political career.

George Bernard Shaw, Irish writer

27

Political Brickbats

He bleeds people. He draws every drop of blood and then drops them from a cliff. He'll blame any person he can put his foot on.

Martha Mitchell, wife of US Attorney General John Mitchell, on President Richard Nixon

The function of socialism is to raise suffering to a higher level.

Norman Mailer, US writer

That dark, designing, sordid, ambitious, vain, proud, arrogant and vindictive knave.

General Charles Lee on US President George Washington

He's a nice guy, but he played too much football with his helmet off.

Lyndon B. Johnson, US President, about Vice President Gerald Ford

29

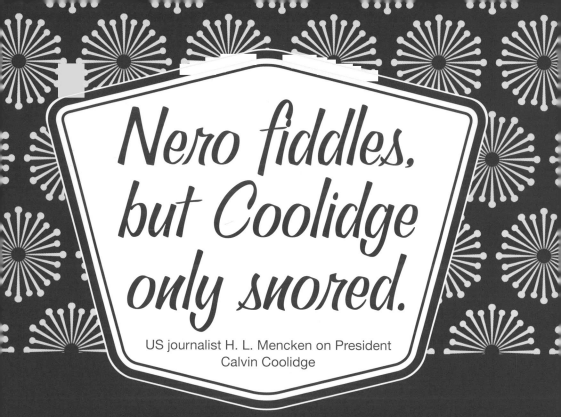

Nero fiddles, but Coolidge only snored.

US journalist H. L. Mencken on President Calvin Coolidge

He didn't care which direction the car was travelling in, so long as he remained in the driver's seat.

Lord Beaverbrook, Anglo-Canadian newspaper tycoon, on British Prime Minister David Lloyd George

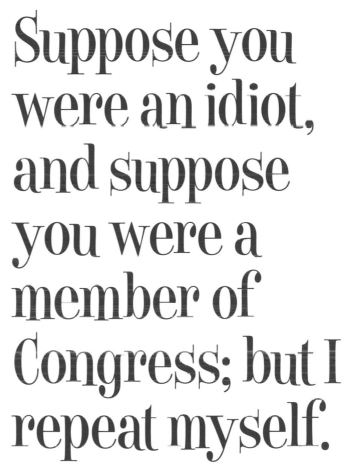

Suppose you were an idiot, and suppose you were a member of Congress; but I repeat myself.

Mark Twain, US writer

Political Brickbats

He bestowed upon the games of golf and bridge all the enthusiasm and perseverance that he withheld from books and ideas.

Emmet Hughes, US writer, on President Dwight Eisenhower

If ignorance goes to $40 a barrel, I want drilling rights to George Bush's head.

Jim Hightower, US liberal political activist, about George Bush, Sr.

We knew George W. Bush was in the oil business - we just didn't know it was snake oil.

James G. Blaine, US politician

His face is ashen, gaunt his whole body. His breath is green with gall. His tongue drops poison.

Ovid, Roman poet (recycled by John Quincy Adams, US President)

I'm like Bush, I see the world more like checkers than chess.

Dennis Miller, US comedian, on US President George W. Bush

Political Brickbats

US Congressman to interviewer Heywood Broun:

I have nothing to say, young man.

Heywood Broun:

I know that. Now shall we get on with the interview?

Give up the PR, and start being a PM!

British Conservative leader David Cameron to Prime Minister Gordon Brown

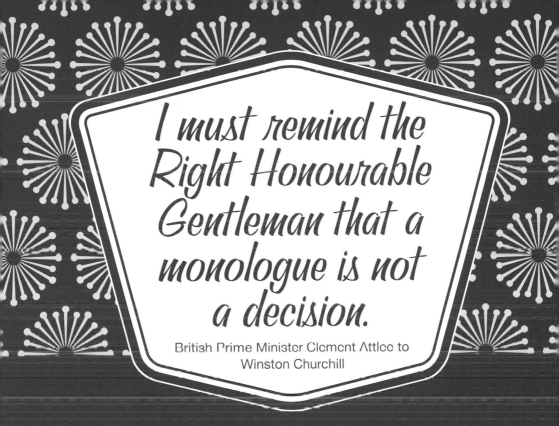

I must remind the Right Honourable Gentleman that a monologue is not a decision.

British Prime Minister Clement Attlee to Winston Churchill

He devoted the best years of his life to preparing his impromptu speeches.

F. E. Smith, British Conservative politician, on Winston Churchill

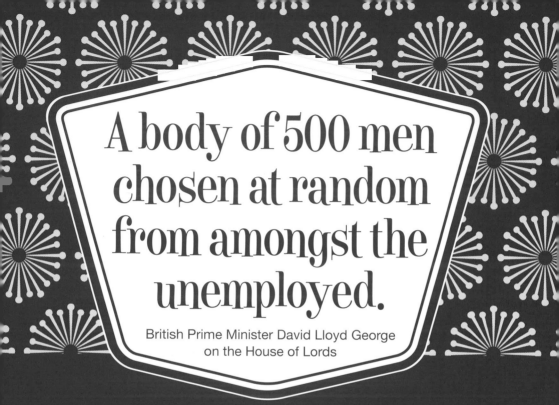

A body of 500 men chosen at random from amongst the unemployed.

British Prime Minister David Lloyd George on the House of Lords

I'm prepared to take advice on leisure from Prince Philip. He's a world expert. He's been practising for most of his adult life.

Neil Kinnock, British Labour Party leader

Politics is too serious to be left to the politicians.

Charles de Gaulle, President of France

His impact on history would be no more than the whiff of scent on a lady's handkerchief.

David Lloyd George, British Prime Minister, on politician Arthur Balfour, who issued the Balfour Declaration in 1917 supporting the establishment of a Jewish homeland

Political Brickbats

A cold-blooded, calculating, unprincipled usurper without a virtue - no statesman.

Thomas Jefferson, US President, on Napoleon Bonaparte, French dictator

I can still remember the first time I ever heard Hubert Humphrey speak. He was in the second hour of a 5-minute talk.

Gerald Ford, US President

Gerald Ford was unknown throughout America. Now he's unknown throughout the world.

US writer Norman Mailer

The battle for the mind of Ronald Reagan was like the trench warfare of World War I: never have so many fought so hard for such barren territory.

Peggy Noonan, US writer

Not a gentleman. Dresses too well.

British philosopher and radical Bertrand Russell on Prime Minister Anthony Eden

Here is a guy who's had a stake driven through his heart and a silver bullet through the forehead for good measure - and yet he keeps coming back.

US broadcaster Ted Koppel on US President Richard Nixon

Do you realise the responsibility I carry? I'm the only person standing between Richard Nixon and the White House.

John F. Kennedy, US President

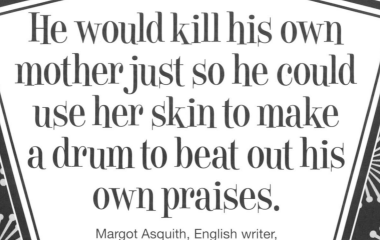

He would kill his own mother just so he could use her skin to make a drum to beat out his own praises.

Margot Asquith, English writer, on Winston Churchill

You have to remember one thing about the will of the people: it wasn't that long ago that we were swept away by the Macarena.

Jon Stewart, US comedian

There have been rumours swirling around Florida that Governor Jeb Bush has been cheating on his wife. But he says no, that's not true - as a Republican, the only people he's been in bed with are the tobacco industry and the gun lobby.

Jay Leno, US comedian and chat show host

A crafty and lecherous old hypocrite whose very statue seems to gloat on the wenches as they walk the States House Yard.

William Cobbett, English pamphleteer, on Benjamin Franklin

My friends are not worth the powder and shot it would take to kill them!

US Senator, Henry Clay

Poor George, he can't help it. He was born with a silver foot in his mouth.

Ann Richards, US politician, on George Bush Sr.

If life were fair, Dan Quayle would be making a living asking, 'Do you want fries with that?'

John Cleese, British actor

If they put the Federal Government in charge of the Sahara Desert, there'd be a shortage of sand within five years.

Milton Friedman, US economist

The Falklands War was a fight between two bald men over a comb.

Jorge Luis Borges, Argentinian writer

There was so little English in that answer, President Chirac would have been happy with it.

William Hague, British Conservative MP, debating with Labour rival John Prescott

Politicians are the same all over. They promise to build a bridge even where there is no river.

Nikita Khrushchev, President of the Communist Party of the Soviet Union

A hotbed of cold feet.

Abba Eban, Israeli diplomat and politician, on the British Foreign Office

More dangerous than a monkey with a razor blade.

Hugo Chavez, Venezuelan Prime Minster, on US President George W. Bush

47

Man will never be free until the last king is strangled with the entrails of the last priest.

Denis Diderot, French philosopher

The oppressed are allowed once every few years to decide which particular representatives of the oppressing class are to represent and repress them.

Karl Marx, German philosopher

The Prime Minister clings to data the way a drunkard clings to lampposts, not for illumination but to keep him standing up.

Romano Prodi, Italian politician, on Italian Prime Minister and media tycoon Silvio Berlusconi

When fascism comes to America, it will be wrapped in the flag and carrying the cross.

US writer Sinclair Lewis

Truman proves the old adage that any man can become President of the United States.

Norman Thomas, US socialist and presidential candidate, on President Harry Truman

A slur upon the moral government of the world.

John Quincy Adams, US President, on his rival Thomas Jefferson

Compared to the Clintons, Reagan is living proof that a Republican with half a brain is better than a Democrat with two.

P. J. O'Rourke, US political satirist

He doesn't dye his hair — he's just prematurely orange.

Gerald Ford, US President, on Ronald Reagan

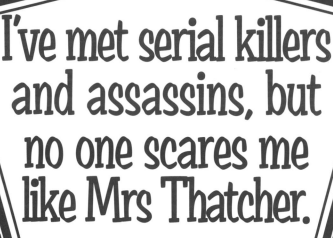

I've met serial killers and assassins, but no one scares me like Mrs Thatcher.

Ken Livingstone, British politician,
on the UK's first woman Prime Minister

Harold Wilson is going round and round the country stirring up apathy.

William Whitelaw, British Conservative politician, on
Labour's leader

Roosevelt proved that a man could be President for life; Truman proved that anybody could be President; and Eisenhower proved that you don't need to have a President at all.

US political commentator Tom Anderson

Nothing more than a well-meaning baboon.

General McClellan, Union General, on US President Abraham Lincoln

> *I don't think Kenneth Baker has his hair cut; he just has an oil change.*
>
> British Labour Party politician on the prominent Conservative MP

The Tories are now so green they're even recycling their leaders.

John Prescott, British Labour MP, on seeing Conservative MP William Hague back on the front bench

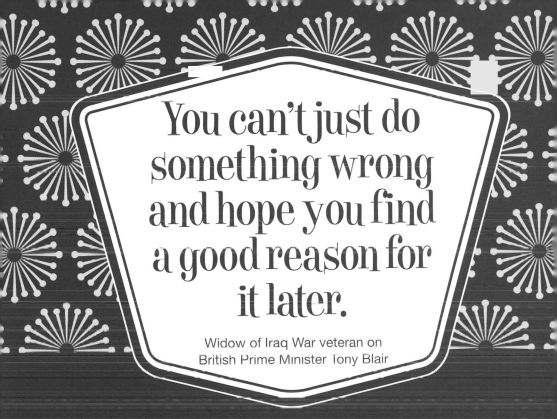

You can't just do something wrong and hope you find a good reason for it later.

Widow of Iraq War veteran on British Prime Minister Tony Blair

Weak, weak, weak.

British Labour leader Tony Blair to Prime Minister John Major

55

Like being mauled by a dead sheep.

Dennis Healey, British Labour Party politician, on Conservative Chancellor Geoffrey Howe's powers of attack

This is a dead parrot... it has ceased to be.

Margaret Thatcher, British Prime Minister, invokes *Monty Python* in mocking the Liberal Democrat Party's new bird emblem

No other President of the United States has ever lied so baldly and so often and so demonstrably.

US political commentator on President George Bush Sr.

His smile is like the silver fittings on a coffin.

Benjamin Disraeli, British Prime Minister, on fellow Tory Robert Peel

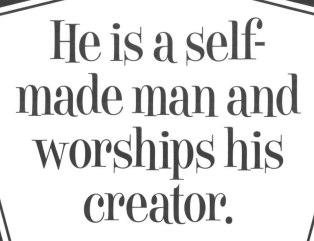

He is a self-made man and worships his creator.

John Bright, British statesman,
on Benjamin Disraeli

When they circumcised Herbert Samuel, they threw away the wrong bit.

David Lloyd George, British Prime Minister, on the Liberal
Home Secretary

If Gladstone fell into the Thames that would be a misfortune. If anybody pulled him out, that, I suppose, would be a calamity.

Benjamin Disraeli, British Prime Minister

Oh, if only I could urinate the way he speaks!

French Prime Minister Georges Clemenceau
on British Prime Minister
David Lloyd George

Political Brickbats

John Major delivers all his statements as though auditioning for the speaking clock.

British Labour Party leader Neil Kinnock on the Conservative Prime Minister

If they will stop telling lies about the Democrats, we will stop telling the truth about them.

Adlai Stevenson, US Vice President, on the Republican party

He looks like an Easter Island statue with a face full of razor blades.

Paul Keating, Australian Prime Minister,
on political rival Jeff Kennett

I would rather be right than be president.

Henry Clay, US Senator

I wouldn't worry. You'll never be either.

Andrew Jackson, US President

John Montagu, Fourth Earl of Sandwich, to John Wilkes, 18th century political reformer:

Sir, I do not know whether you will die on the gallows or of the pox!

Wilkes:

That, sir, depends on whether I first embrace your Lordship's principles or your Lordship's mistresses.

He looks like he may have sat on a corncob.

British Conservative MP Alan Clark on cabinet colleague Douglas Hurd

Debating with him is like being flogged by a warm lettuce.

Australian Prime Minister Paul Keating on political rival John Howard

He's like a lizard on a rock, alive but looking dead.

Australian Prime Minister Paul Keating on political rival John Howard

Political Brickbats

What goes around, comes around. Trump's top policy adviser, Stephen Miller, has called out an "angry, vindictive person" whose "grotesque comments are so out of touch with reality." While everyone will assume he's talking about his boss, Miller was actually chiding Steve Bannon. Which is like Saruman berating Gollum for not being nicer to baby Hobbits.

Michael R. Burch aka "The Loyal Opposition"

Classic
Put-downs

Having
A Pop

Hollywood is a place where people from Iowa mistake each other for stars.

Fred Allen, US comedian

I'm glad he has finally found his true love – what a pity he can't marry himself.

US singer Frank Sinatra on film star Robert Redford

Dramatic art in her opinion is knowing how to fill a sweater.

US actress Bette Davis about rival actress Jayne Mansfield

He's in danger of waking up one morning in his own arms.

US actress Mamie Van Doren on Warren Beatty

There goes that famous good time that was had by all.

US actress Bette Davis
on a struggling actress
of her day

Who can forget Mel Gibson in Hamlet? Though many have tried.

Harry Andrews, British actor

After Braveheart, they said he'd never make a true Scotsman, but look at him now – alcoholic and racist.

Frankie Boyle, Scottish comedian, on Mel Gibson

Having A Pop

Pierce Brosnan reminds me of the models in knitwear magazines.

Paul Hoggart, British journalist

Elizabeth Taylor has more chins than the Chinese telephone directory.

Joan Rivers, US comedian

A wide screen just makes a terrible movie twice as bad.

Samuel Goldwyn, US film producer

Jamie Lee Curtis has trouble learning her lines because English is not her first language. She doesn't unfortunately have a first language.

John Cleese, British actor

She has breasts of granite and a mind like a Gruyère cheese.

Billy Wilder, Austrian screenwriter and director, on Marilyn Monroe

The only moving thing about Charlton Heston's performance was his wig.

Michael Coveney, British film critic

His acting is so bad, even his impersonation of a drunk is unconvincing.

Critic Harry Medved on Dean Martin

Peter Sellers was his own worst enemy, although there was plenty of competition.

Ray Boulting, British film producer and director

You had to stand in line to hate him.

US gossip columnist Hedda Hopper on Columbia Pictures president Harry Cohn

In order to feel safer on his private jet, John Travolta has purchased a bomb-sniffing dog. Unfortunately, the dog arrived six movies too late.

Tina Fey, US comedian

How difficult can it be to fly an airplane? I mean, John Travolta learned how...

Graham Chapman, English comedian

I remember my brother saying he'd like to marry Elizabeth Taylor. My father said, 'Don't worry, son, your time will come.'

Spike Milligan, Anglo-Irish comedian

It was like kissing the Berlin Wall.

Helena Bonham-Carter, British actress, on kissing Woody Allen, US writer-director, in the film *Mighty Aphrodite*

Dear Ingrid. Speaks five languages and can't act in any of them.

British actor Sir John Gielgud, about Ingrid Bergman

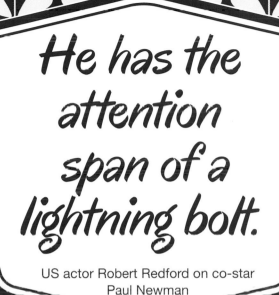

He has the attention span of a lightning bolt.

US actor Robert Redford on co-star
Paul Newman

Every minute this broad spends
outside of bed is a waste of time.

British producer Michael Todd on Elizabeth Taylor

A man of many talents ... all of them minor.

Leslie Halliwell, British film critic, on director Blake Edwards

A buxom milkmaid reminiscent of a cow wearing a girdle, and both have the same amount of acting talent.

Mr Blackwell, US fashion critic, about Brigitte Bardot

Liz Hurley longs for the day when people stop pointing cameras at her. Speaking as someone who has seen all her films, I couldn't agree more.

Jonathan Ross, British talk show host

I didn't know her well, but after watching her in action I didn't want to know her well.

US actress Joan Crawford on Judy Garland

Dry and draughty, like an abandoned temple.

Truman Capote, US writer, on Greta Garbo

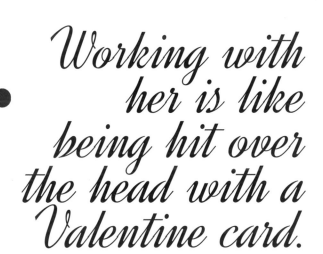

Working with her is like being hit over the head with a Valentine card.

Christopher Plummer, Canadian actor, on Julie Andrews

Acting is the most minor of gifts and not a very high-class way to earn a living. After all, Shirley Temple could do it at the age of four.

Katharine Hepburn, US actress

She ran the gamut of emotions from A to B.

Dorothy Parker, US writer, on Katharine Hepburn

There are two things I would never do – climb Mount Everest and work with Val Kilmer again.

John Frankenheimer, US film director

I like Warren. I think he's talented. He's just not fun to be with.

Robert Altman, US writer and director, on Warren Beatty

There was no one remotely like John Houston, except maybe Lucifer.

Doris Lilly, US gossip columnist

They asked Jack Benny to do something for the Actor's Orphanage, so he shot both his parents and moved in.

Bob Hope, British comedian

Having A Pop

Joan always cries a lot. Her tear ducts must be close to her bladder.

US actress Bette Davis on Joan Crawford

Miss Davis was always partial to covering up her face in motion pictures. She called it 'Art'. Others might call it camouflage - a cover-up for the absence of any real beauty.

US actress Joan Crawford on Bette Davis

Bette likes to rant and rave. I just sit and knit. She yelled and I knitted a scarf from Hollywood to Malibu.

US actress Joan Crawford on Bette Davis

Wet she was a star. Dry she ain't.

Joe Pasternak, US film producer, on swimmer and actress Esther Williams

Kirk would be the first to tell you that he's a difficult man; I'd be the second.

US actor Burt Lancaster on Kirk Douglas

Having A Pop

Silicon from the knees up.

George Masters, Hollywood stylist, on actress Raquel Welch

Elizabeth Taylor's so fat, she puts mayonnaise on an aspirin.

Joan Rivers, US comedian

It's like kissing Hitler.

US actor Tony Curtis on kissing co-star Marilyn Monroe

Stars 'The Rock', but 'The Wood' might be a better description of his performance.

Peter Rainer, US screenwriter, on wrestler-turned-actor The Rock

Where some men are self-contained he's vacuum-packed.

US actor Anthony Perkins on fellow actor Steven Segal

You always knew where you were with Errol. He always let you down.

David Niven, British actor, on Errol Flynn

The best time I ever had with Joan Crawford was when I pushed her down the stairs in *Whatever Happened to Baby Jane?*

US actress Bette Davis on her co-star in *Whatever Happened to Baby Jane?*

Most of the time he sounds like he has a mouth full of wet toilet paper.

Rex Reed, US film critic, on Marlon Brando

He's the kind of guy that when he dies, he's going up to heaven and give God a bad time for making him bald.

Marlon Brando, US actor, on Frank Sinatra

And to hell it can go!

Ed Naha, US writer and producer, on the 1959 film *From Hell It Came*

It proves what Harry always said: 'Give the public what they want and they'll come out for it.'

US comedian Red Skelton commenting on the size of the turn-out for the funeral of Harry Cohn, head of Columbia Picture Studios

Louis B. Meyer's arm around your shoulder meant his hand was closer to your throat.

Jules Dassin, US film director

I would openly celebrate Quentin Tarantino's death.

Don Murphy, US film producer

God felt sorry for actors, so he created Hollywood to give them a place in the sun and a swimming pool. The price they had to pay was to surrender their talents.

Cedric Hardwicke, English actor

The movies are the only business where you can go out front and applaud yourself.

Will Rogers, US actor

You can pick out actors by the glazed look that comes into their eyes when the conversation wanders away from themselves.

Michael Wilding, English actor

The average Hollywood film star's ambition is to be admired by an American, courted by an Italian, married to an Englishman and have a French boyfriend.

Katharine Hepburn, US actress

Having A Pop

I once bumped into Sally Field by the pool in a big Hollywood hotel, and time, it must be said, had not been kind to the former screen goddess - in fact, it hadn't even been mildly understanding.

Dylan Jones, British journalist

I've done my bit for motion pictures; I've stopped making them.

Liberace, US musician

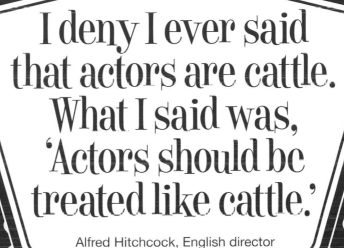

I deny I ever said that actors are cattle. What I said was, 'Actors should be treated like cattle.'

Alfred Hitchcock, English director

I pity the French cinema because it has no money. I pity the American cinema because it has no ideas.

Jean-Luc Godard, French director

An extremely mean and deeply heartless figure.

Peter Willes, actor and film and television director, on actor David Niven

An over-fat, flatulent 62-year-old windbag, a master of inconsequence now masquerading as guru, passing off his vast limitations as pious virtues.

Irish actor Richard Harris on fellow actor Michael Caine

If you'd been any prettier it would have been *Florence of Arabia.*

English playwright Noël Coward
to actor Peter O'Toole

She has discovered the secret of perpetual middle age.

Oscar Levant, US musician and comedian, about Zsa Zsa Gabor

Television has raised writing to a new low.

Sam Goldwyn, US film producer

I'm here to speak about his wit, his charm, his warmth, his talent ... at last, a real acting job!

US actor Burt Lancaster on fellow actor Kirk Douglas

Work hard. Save your money. When you have enough money saved, buy an axe. Use it to chop off your head and stop bothering me.

US actor Lionel Barrymore to an aspiring actor who asked for advice

Flo:
Well, I've never been so insulted in my life.
Hackenbush:
(Looking at his watch) Well, it's early yet.

US comedian Groucho Marx, *A Day at the Races*

Tina Turner, all legs and hair and a mouth that could swallow this whole stadium, including the hot dog stand.

Laura Dee Davies, US music critic

The truth is that Michael Jackson's album was called *Bad* because there wasn't enough room on the sleeve for *Pathetic*.

The artist formerly known as Prince

I'm a fan of hers, back when she was popular.

US singer Mariah Carey on Madonna

She is so hairy, when she lifted up her arm, I thought it was Tina Turner in her armpit.

US comedian Joan Rivers on Madonna

She's as dim as a lightbulb in a power cut.

English music manager
Sharon Osbourne on Dannii Minogue

She ought to be arrested for loitering in front of an orchestra.

Bette Midler, US singer and actress, about singer and actress Helen Reddy

When you talk to him, he looks at you and grins and grins and nods and nods and appears to be the world's best listener, until you realize that he is not listening at all.

Larry King, US television host, on country singer Willie Nelson

Artists aren't really people. I'm actually 40 per cent papier mâché.

Morrissey, The Smiths

He moves like a parody between a majorette girl and Fred Astaire.

US writer Truman Capote on Mick Jagger

I've never had a problem with drugs. I've only had problems with the police.

Keith Richards, English guitarist

It's like a monkey with arthritis trying to go on stage and look young.

Sir Elton John, British musician, on Keith Richards

A cross between an aardvark and an albino rat.

US record producer John Simon describes Barbra Streisand

Every time I see Bono in those big fly glasses and tight leather pants I just can't hack it. I can't see that as solving the world's problems. He's crushing his testicles in tight trousers for world peace.

John Lydon, British singer

When an opera star sings her head off, it usually improves her appearance.

Victor Borge, Danish-American musician and comedian

Wagner has beautiful moments but awful quarters of an hour.

Gioacchino Antonio Rossini, Italian composer

Wagner's music is better than it sounds.

Mark Twain, US writer

According to Britney Spears' pre-nup agreement, after she divorces Kevin Federline she'll have to pay him thirty thousand dollars a month. When you add that to Kevin Federline's other sources of income, he'll be making a total of thirty thousand dollars a month.

Conan O'Brien, US talk show host

Whenever I think about Atomic Kitten I'm saddened because I think there's a supermarket somewhere in the north of England that's three girls short.

Jimmy Carr, British comic, on a briefly successful girl band

The closest thing to Roseanne Barr's singing the national anthem was my cat being neutered.

Johnny Carson, US comedian and TV host

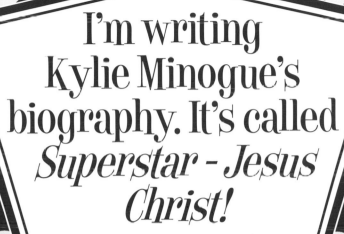

I'm writing Kylie Minogue's biography. It's called *Superstar - Jesus Christ!*

Barry Cryer, British comic writer

Music journalists like Elvis Costello because music journalists look like Elvis Costello.

US rock star David Lee Roth on media tastes

Whoever told Simon Cowell he had ears? He can't even dress properly. People who should be selling fruit and veg are talking about art, and music is art.

Boy George, British singer

Hell is full of musical amateurs.

George Bernard Shaw, Irish playwright

Well, I only hope he saved some of my money to pay for his funeral.

Maria Callas, Greek opera singer, on hearing of the death of her agent

I didn't meet Chris Martin... he met me.

Ian McCulloch, Echo and the Bunnymen, on the Coldplay frontman

Having A Pop

This is a fault common to all singers: that among their friends they never are inclined to sing when they are asked; unasked, they never desist.

Horace, Roman lyric poet, *Satires* Book I

Her voice sounded like an eagle being goosed.

Ralph Novak, US guitar maker on Yoko Ono

If I found her floating in my pool, I'd punish my dog.

Joan Rivers, US comedian, about Yoko Ono

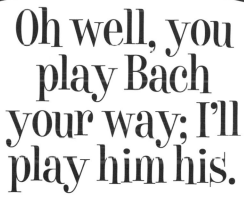

Oh well, you play Bach your way; I'll play him his.

Wanda Landowska, Polish harpsichordist, to a fellow musician

Last night at Carnegie Hall, Jack Benny played Mendelssohn. Mendelssohn lost.

Harold C. Schonberg, US music critic

Having A Pop

Michael is claiming racism. And I say ... honey, you've got to pick a race first. All of a sudden, you're a black man, then you're Diana Ross, now you're Audrey Hepburn.

Robin Williams, US comedian, on Michael Jackson

Michael Jackson was a poor black boy who grew up to be a rich white woman.

Molly Ivins, US columnist

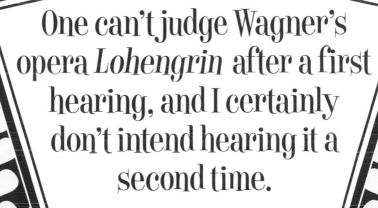

One can't judge Wagner's opera *Lohengrin* after a first hearing, and I certainly don't intend hearing it a second time.

Gioacchino Antonio Rossini, Italian composer

A composer for one right hand.

German composer Richard Wagner on Polish composer Frédéric Chopin

Canadians have a health care system based on treating hockey injuries and curing sinus infections that come from trying to pronounce too many French vowels.

P. J. O'Rourke, US political satirist

I don't even know what street Canada is on.

Al Capone, US mobster

Belgium is the best remedy against patriotism.

Geert van Istendaelm, Belgian writer

Having A Pop

The food is excellent. The beer is cold. The sun nearly always shines. There is coffee on every corner. Rupert Murdoch no longer lives there. Life doesn't get much better than this.

Bill Bryson, US author on Australia

Belgium is just a country invented by the British to annoy the French.

General de Gaulle, French President

The Australian book of etiquette and good manners is a very slim volume.

Paul Theroux, US travel writer

France is a dog-hole.

William Shakespeare, English playwright, *All's Well That Ends Well*

Having A Pop

Scotland is a marvellous place, but there's nobody there!

Billy Connolly, Scottish comedian

A Scotsman keeps the Sabbath and every other thing he can lay his hands on.

Samuel Johnson, English writer

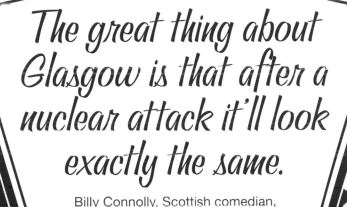

The great thing about Glasgow is that after a nuclear attack it'll look exactly the same.

Billy Connolly, Scottish comedian, on his home town

If it was raining soup, the Irish would go out with forks.

Brendan Behan, Irish writer

A Canadian is someone who knows how to make love in a canoe.

Pierre Berton, Canadian writer

God Bless America, but God help Canada to put up with them.

Canadian saying

In Italy for thirty years under the Borgias they had warfare, terror, murder and bloodshed but they produced Michelangelo, Leonardo da Vinci and the Renaissance. In Switzerland, they had brotherly love; they had five hundred years of democracy and peace and what did that produce? The cuckoo clock.

Orson Welles, US director, *The Third Man*

Apart from cheese and tulips, the main product of Holland is advocaat, a drink made from lawyers.

Alan Coren, English writer

Switzerland is a place where they don't like to fight, so they get people to do their fighting for them while they ski and eat chocolate.

Larry David, US actor and comedian

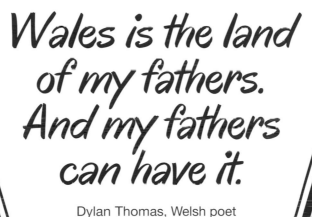

Wales is the land of my fathers. And my fathers can have it.

Dylan Thomas, Welsh poet

There are still parts of Wales where the only concession to gaiety is a striped shroud.

Gwyn Thomas, Welsh writer

One German a beer, two Germans an organization, three Germans a war.

Polish saying

There is nothing on earth more terrible than English music, except English painting.

Heinrich Heine, German poet, writer and literary critic

Poor Mexico, so far from God and so near to the United States.

Porfirio Díaz, President of Mexico

The Americans, like the English, probably make love worse than any other race.

Walt Whitman, US writer

Well ... I suppose you gotta live somewhere.

Suggested motto for Cleveland, Ohio, but can be adapted

Last week, I went to Philadelphia, but it was closed.

W. C. Fields, US comedian

Irish writer Oscar Wilde To French actress Sarah Bernhardt:

Do you mind if I smoke?

Sarah Bernhardt:

I don't care if you burn.

A woman is only a woman. But a good cigar is a smoke.

Rudyard Kipling, English writer, later re-used by US comedian Groucho Marx

The trouble with her is that she lacks the power of conversation, but not the power of speech.

George Bernard Shaw, Irish playwright

His mother should have thrown him away and kept the stork.

US actress Mae West in *Belle of the Nineties*

Hamlet *is a coarse and barbarous play ... the product of a drunken savage.*

Voltaire, French writer,
on William Shakespeare,
English playwright

Lady Astor to Winston Churchill:

Sir, if you were my husband, I would poison your drink.

Churchill in response:

Madam, if you were my wife, I would drink it.

Elegant Insults

Why don't you write books people can read?

Nora Joyce to her husband, Irish writer, James Joyce

Jazz isn't dead. It just smells funny.

Frank Zappa, US musician

He is not only dull himself; he is the cause of dullness in others.

Samuel Johnson, English writer

Many people would no more think of entering journalism than the sewage business, which at least does us some good.

Stephen Fry, British actor and comedian

They never open their mouths without subtracting from the sum of human knowledge.

Thomas Brackett Reed, US politician

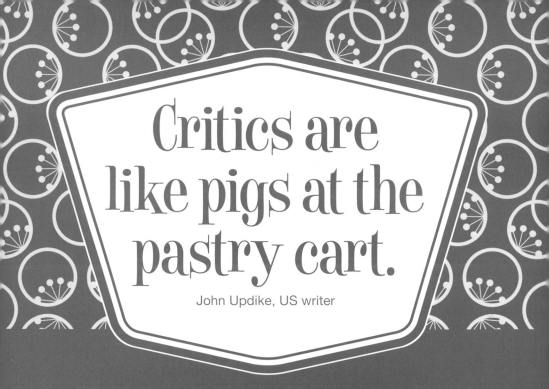

Critics are like pigs at the pastry cart.

John Updike, US writer

I am reading Henry James ... and feel myself as one entombed in a block of smooth amber.

Virginia Woolf, English writer

The last time I was in Spain I got through six Jeffrey Archer novels. I must remember to take enough toilet paper next time.

Bob Monkhouse, English comedian

Mr Henry James writes fiction as if it were a painful duty.

Oscar Wilde, Irish writer

I remember the astonishment I felt when I first read Shakespeare. I felt an irresistible repulsion and tedium.

Leo Tolstoy, Russian writer

He is the same old sausage, fizzing and sputtering in his own grease.

US writer Henry James on Scottish philosopher Thomas Carlyle

A great cow, full of ink.

French writer Gustave Flaubert on writer
George Sand

His style has the desperate jauntiness of an orchestra fiddling away for dear life on a sinking ship.

US writer Edmund Wilson on Evelyn Waugh

He writes his plays for the ages – the ages between five and twelve.

US drama critic George Nathan about George Bernard Shaw

A lewd vegetarian.

Charles Kingsley on fellow English poet Percy Bysshe Shelley

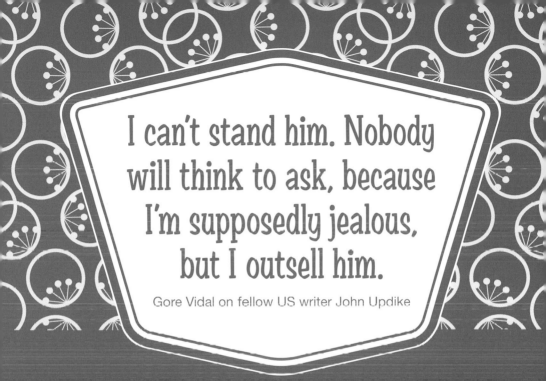

I can't stand him. Nobody will think to ask, because I'm supposedly jealous, but I outsell him.

Gore Vidal on fellow US writer John Updike

He's a full-fledged housewife from Kansas with all the prejudices.

Gore Vidal, US writer, about Truman Capote

141

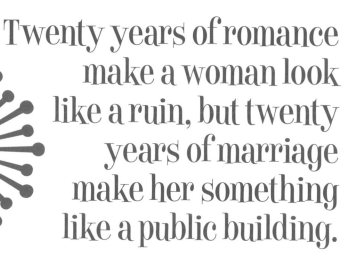

Twenty years of romance make a woman look like a ruin, but twenty years of marriage make her something like a public building.

Oscar Wilde, Irish writer

Love: a temporary insanity curable by marriage.

Ambrose Bierce, US journalist

I expect Women will be the last thing civilized by Man.

George Meredith, English novelist

She should get a divorce and settle down.

Jack Paar, US author and comedian, on Zsa Zsa Gabor

A fat flabby little person with the face of a baker.

French writer Victor de Balabin on French novelist Honoré de Balzac

A little emasculated mass of inanity.

Theodore Roosevelt, US President, about Henry James

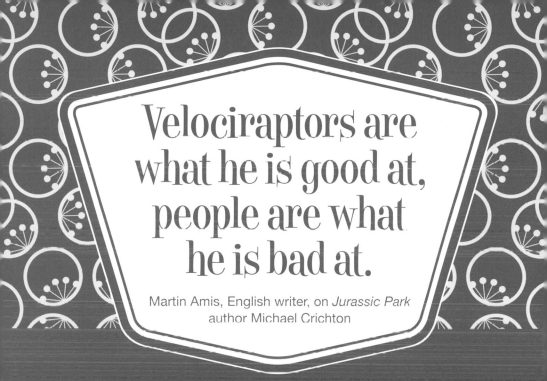

Velociraptors are what he is good at, people are what he is bad at.

Martin Amis, English writer, on *Jurassic Park* author Michael Crichton

His ignorance covers the world like a blanket, and there's scarcely a hole in it anywhere.

Mark Twain, US writer

Elegant Insults

The godless arch scoundrel Voltaire is dead - dead like a dog, like a beast.

Wolfgang Amadeus Mozart, Austrian composer

I didn't attend the funeral but I sent a nice letter saying I approved of it.

Mark Twain, US writer

As to Hemingway, I read him, something about bells and bulls, and loathed it.

Vladimir Nabokov, Russian novelist

He has never been known to use a word that might send the reader to a dictionary.

US writer William Faulkner on Ernest Hemingway

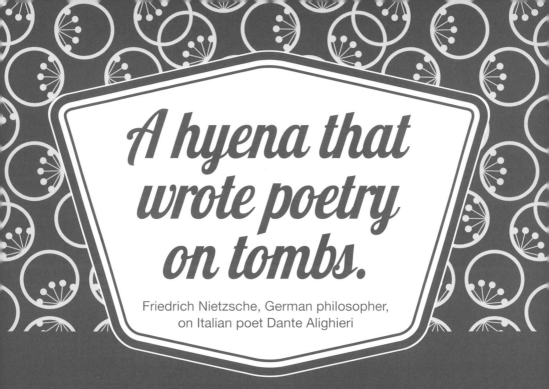

A hyena that wrote poetry on tombs.

Friedrich Nietzsche, German philosopher,
on Italian poet Dante Alighieri

She preserved to the age of fifty-six that contempt for
ideas which is normal among boys and girls of fifteen.

Odell Shepherd, US professor, poet and politician, about novelist
Louisa May Alcott

The wreck of Stevenson floating about in the slipslop of Henry James.

Irish critic George Moore on writer Joseph Conrad

A huge pendulum attached to a small clock.

Ivan Panin, Russian critic, on English poet Samuel Taylor Coleridge

Fine words! I wonder where you stole them.

Jonathan Swift, Anglo-Irish satirist

He was one of the nicest old ladies I ever met.

William Faulkner, US writer, about Henry James

George Bernard Shaw: the spinster aunt of English literature.

Kenneth Tynan, English theatre critic

With the single exception of Homer, there is no eminent writer, not even Sir Walter Scott, whom I can despise so entirely as I despise Shakespeare.

George Bernard Shaw, Irish playwright

He writes like a Pakistani who learned English when he was twelve years old in order to become a chartered accountant.

English playwright John Osborne on George Bernard Shaw

I am enclosing two tickets to my new play; bring a friend ... if you have one.

Irish playwright George Bernard Shaw to Winston Churchill

Cannot possibly attend first night, will attend second night ... if there is one.

Churchill's reply to George Bernard Shaw

Winston Churchill (to the Duchess of York):
My dear, would you consider sleeping with me if I were to offer you The Hope Diamond?

The Duchess of York:
Oh, Mr Churchill, you're such a romantic!

Winston Churchill:
Well then, would you consider sleeping with me for 10 pounds?

The Duchess of York:
My dear sir, what sort of woman do you take me for?

Winston Churchill:
I believe we've already established that. Now we're simply haggling over the price.

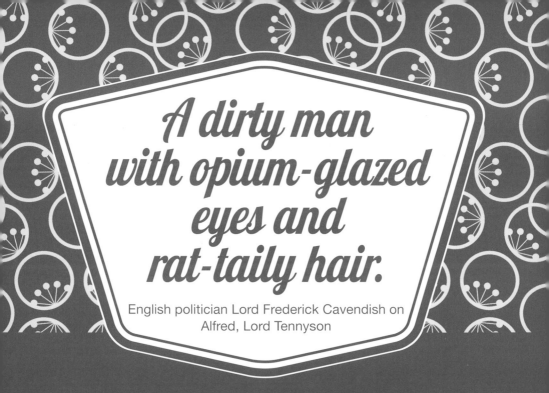

A dirty man with opium-glazed eyes and rat-taily hair.

English politician Lord Frederick Cavendish on Alfred, Lord Tennyson

He has sat on the fence so long that the iron has entered his soul.

David Lloyd George, British Prime Minister

The best view of London is from the National Theatre, because from there you can't see the National Theatre.

Adapted from Oscar Wilde's famous comment about Paris and the Eiffel Tower

You're a parasite for sore eyes.

Gregory Ratoff, US actor and director

So boring that you fall asleep halfway through her name.

British writer Alan Bennett on journalist Arianna Stassinopoulos (now Huffington)

Art produces ugly things which frequently become beautiful with time. Fashion, on the other hand, produces beautiful things which always become ugly with time.

Jean Cocteau, French poet, novelist, playwright and film-maker

A bunch of lunatics and a woman.

Art critic at the first Impressionist exhibition in 1874

All critics should be assassinated.

Man Ray, US artist

Junk masquerading as art.

Critic on British artist Tracey Emin's award-winning
installation art

When you go to the mind reader, do you get half price?

David Letterman, US talk show host

While he was not dumber than an ox he was not any smarter either.

James Thurber, US writer

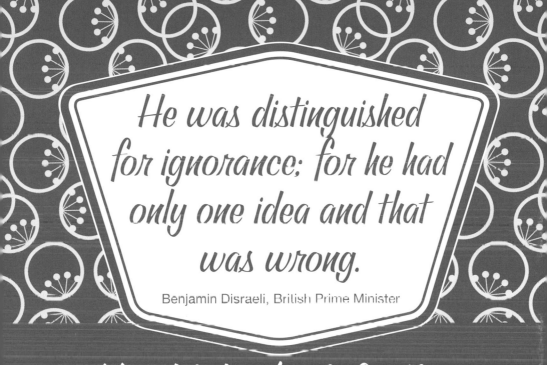

He was distinguished for ignorance; for he had only one idea and that was wrong.

Benjamin Disraeli, British Prime Minister

He thinks by infection, catching an opinion like a cold.

John Ruskin, English writer, speaking of the common man

159

Moby-Dick *is sad stuff, dull and dreary, and his Mad Captain is a monstrous bore.*

The Southern Quarterly Review, 1851, on Hermann Melville's Moby-Dick

Thank you for sending me a copy of your book; I'll waste no time reading it.

Moses Hadas, US scholar

Fifty years from now our children will wonder what their ancestors could have meant by naming Dickens as a top novelist of his day.

Sunday Review, London, 1858

This is not a novel to be tossed aside lightly. It should be thrown with great force.

Dorothy Parker, US writer

Elegant Insults

Nazi ambassador to France, to spanish artist Pablo Picasso, on seeing his painting 'Guernica', which depicts the bombing of the spanish town:

Oh, it was you, Monsieur Picasso, who did that?

Pablo Picasso:

No, it was you.

How vain painting is - we admire the realistic depiction of objects which in their original state we don't admire at all.

Blaise Pascal, French writer, scientist and philosopher

A skilful but short-lived decorator.

Edgar Degas, French artist, on painter Claude Monet

He will never be anything but a dauber.

Titian on fellow Italian artist Tintoretto

Dada's art is just turpentine intoxication.

Marcel Duchamp, French artist

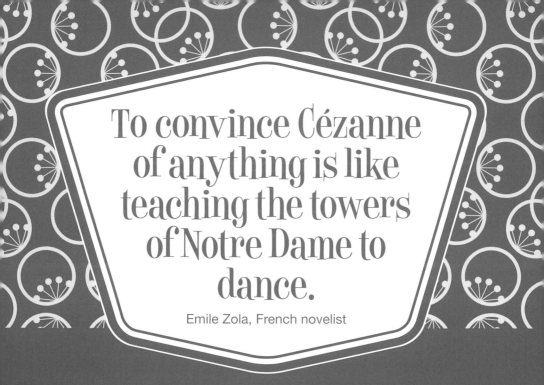

To convince Cézanne of anything is like teaching the towers of Notre Dame to dance.

Emile Zola, French novelist

As for M. Cézanne, his name will be forever linked with the most memorable artistic joke of the last fifteen years.

Camille Macular, French art critic, on French artist Paul Cézanne

That woman speaks eighteen languages, and can't say No in any of them.

Dorothy Parker, US writer

If all the young ladies who attended the Yale prom were laid end to end, no one would be the least surprised.

Dorothy Parker, US writer

She looked as though butter wouldn't melt in her mouth - or anywhere else.

Elsa Lanchester, English-American actress

In order to avoid being called a flirt, she always yielded easily.

Talleyrand, French diplomat

She has been kissed as often as a police-court Bible, and by much the same class of people.

Robertson Davies, Canadian writer

She proceeds to dip her little fountain-pen filler into pots of oily venom and to squirt the mixture at all her friends.

Harold Nicholson, English diplomat and writer, on society hostess Mrs Ronnie Greville

Elegant Insults

We doubt ... whether this is the right point of view from which to criticize the political situation at the present time.

US playwright T. S. Eliot, then a Faber & Faber editor, rejecting George Orwell's *Animal Farm* for publication in Britain in 1944

There is not much demand for animal stories in the USA.

Dial Press, turning down *Animal Farm* in 1944

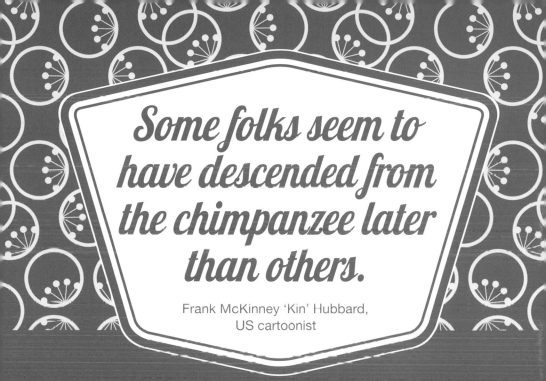

Some folks seem to have descended from the chimpanzee later than others.

Frank McKinney 'Kin' Hubbard,
US cartoonist

That's not writing, that's typing.

Truman Capote, US writer, on Jack Kerouac

Elegant Insults

It is becoming painfully evident that Mr James has written himself out as far as novel-writing is concerned!

US literary critic William Morton Payne, writing in *The Dial* in 1884 on Henry James

What other culture could have produced someone like Hemingway and not seen the joke?

Gore Vidal, US writer

Walt Whitman is as unacquainted with art as a hog is with mathematics.

The London Critic, 1855

Today's public figures can no longer write their own speeches or books, and there is some evidence that they can't read them either.

Gore Vidal, US writer

I mistook his silences for intelligence.

Bianca Jagger, Nicaraguan social and human rights activist, on US artist Andy Warhol

He has all of the virtues I dislike and none of the vices I admire.

Winston Churchill, British Prime Minister

The trouble is that the stupid people - who constitute the grand overwhelming majority of this and all other nations - do believe and are moulded and convinced by what they get out of a newspaper.

Mark Twain, US writer

I worship the quicksand he walks in.

Art Buchwald, US humorist

M. Flaubert n'est pas un ecrivain. (Mr Flaubert is not a writer)

Review of *Madame Bovary* in *Le Figaro*, 1857

If length be not considered a merit ... *Paradise Lost* has no other.

English poet Edmund Waller on John Milton's epic work in 1680

There is nothing wrong with you that reincarnation won't cure.

Jack E Leonard, US comedian

They don't hardly make 'em like him any more - but just to be on the safe side, he should be castrated anyway.

Hunter S. Thompson, US writer

Elegant Insults

I finished *Ulysses* and think it is a mis-fire ... The book is diffuse. It is brackish. It is pretentious. It is underbred, not only in the obvious sense, but in the literary sense. A first-rate writer, I mean, respects writing too much to be tricky.

English writer Virginia Woolf in her diary, September 6, 1922, on James Joyce's classic *Ulysses*

He has delusions of adequacy.

Walter Kerr, US theatre critic

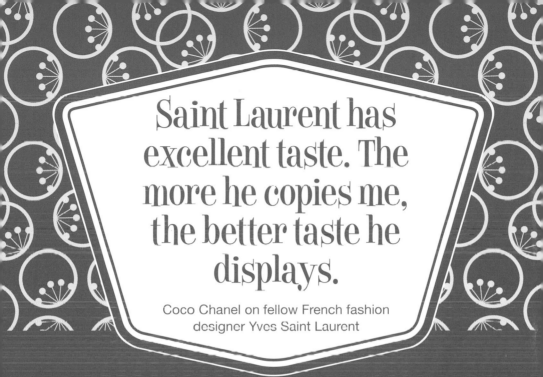

Saint Laurent has excellent taste. The more he copies me, the better taste he displays.

Coco Chanel on fellow French fashion designer Yves Saint Laurent

He loves nature despite what it did to him.

Forrest Tucker, US actor

She sounded like the Book of Revelations read out over a railway station public address system by a headmistress of a certain age wearing calico knickers.

Australian author and critic Clive James on Margaret Thatcher

She spends her day powdering her face till she looks like a bled pig.

Margot Asquith, British socialite and writer

A period novel about the Civil War! Who needs it - who cares?

Editor turning down the offer to serialize *Gone With The Wind* (1936)

We cannot name one considerable poem of his that is likely to remain upon the thresh-floor of fame.

London Weekly Review on English poet Samuel Taylor Coleridge

Why was I born with such contemporaries?

Oscar Wilde, Irish writer

The musician is perhaps the most modest of animals, but he is also the proudest. It is he who invented the sublime art of ruining poetry.

Erik Satie, French composer

How can they tell?

US writer Dorothy Parker when she heard that US President Calvin Coolidge had died

She's the sort of person who lives for others; you can tell the others by their haunted expression.

Irish novelist C. S. Lewis, from *The Screwtape Letters*

Curious thing, plain women are always jealous of their husbands, beautiful women never are!

Oscar Wilde, Irish writer

She looked as if she had been poured into her clothes and had forgotten to say 'when'.

P. G. Wodehouse, British writer

He is simply a shiver looking for a spine to run up.

Paul Keating, Australian Prime Minister

He was so narrow-minded he could see through a keyhole with both eyes.

Molly Ivins, US columnist

The Prime Minister tells us she has given the French President a piece of her mind, not a gift I would receive with alacrity...

English politician Denis Healey on Margaret Thatcher

It's exciting to have a real crisis on your hands, when you have spent half your political life dealing with humdrum issues like the environment.

Margaret Thatcher, British Prime Minister, on the Falklands War

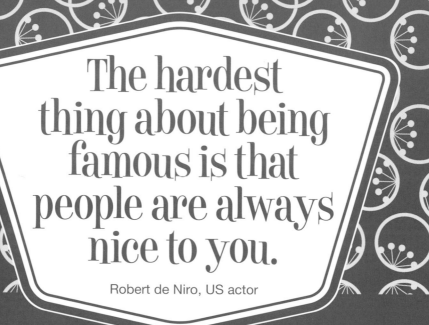

The hardest thing about being famous is that people are always nice to you.

Robert de Niro, US actor

If your brains were dynamite, there wouldn't be enough to blow your hat off.

Kurt Vonnegut, US writer, *Timequake*

I go to the theatre to be entertained ... I don't want to see plays about rape, sodomy and drug addiction ... I can get all that at home.

Peter Cook, British comedian

Sometimes I need what only you can provide: your absence.

Ashleigh Brilliant, British author and cartoonist

Treachery with a smile on its face.

Margaret Thatcher, British Prime Minister, on being removed from office by her own party

Happiness is having a large, loving, caring, close-knit family in another city.

George Burns, US comedian

From the moment I picked your book up until I laid it down, I convulsed with laughter. Some day I intend reading it.

Groucho Marx, US comedian

She said she was approaching forty, and I couldn't help wondering from what direction.

Bob Hope, US comedian

Elegant Insults

You don't reach Downing Street by pretending you've travelled the road to Damascus when you haven't even left home.

Margaret Thatcher, British Prime Minister, on Labour Party leader Neil Kinnock

What's on your mind? If you'll forgive the overstatement.

Fred Allen, US comedian

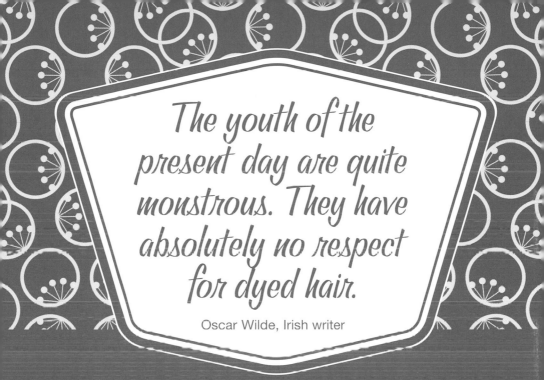

The youth of the present day are quite monstrous. They have absolutely no respect for dyed hair.

Oscar Wilde, Irish writer

If you want to know what God thinks of money, just look at the people he gave it to.

Dorothy Parker, US writer

Woman have many faults. Men have only two: everything they say, and everything they do.

Anonymous

You have delighted us long enough.

Jane Austen, English author

Classic
Put-downs

Military
Mockery

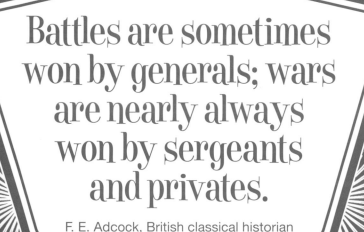

Battles are sometimes won by generals; wars are nearly always won by sergeants and privates.

F. E. Adcock, British classical historian

Soldiers usually win the battles and generals get the credit for them.

Napoleon Bonaparte, French dictator

When the rich wage war, it's the poor who die.

Jean-Paul Sartre, French philosopher

War does not determine who is right – only who is left.

Bertrand Russell, British philosopher

Military Mockery

You can't destroy the Polish national consciousness or Poles on the battlefield, but if you give them power, they will destroy themselves.

Otto von Bismarck, German statesman

People sleep peaceably in their beds at night only because rough men stand ready to do violence on their behalf.

George Orwell, English author

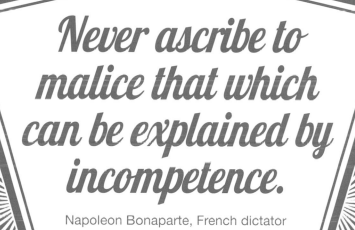

Never ascribe to malice that which can be explained by incompetence.

Napoleon Bonaparte, French dictator

I have an intellect that is badly missed in the country which is run by generals and colonels.

Garry Kasparov, Russian chess grandmaster

Military Mockery

If he was not a great man, he was at least a great poster.

Margot Asquith, British socialite and writer, speaking about Field Marshal Lord Kitchener who appeared on First World War posters with the message 'Your Country Needs You'

All very successful commanders are prima donnas and must be so treated.

George S. Patton, US General

Being in the army is like being in the Boy Scouts, except that the Boy Scouts have adult supervision.

Blake Clark, US actor and Vietnam veteran

Children play soldiers. That makes sense. But why do soldiers play children?

Karl Kraus, Austrian writer

Military Mockery

He was always backing into the limelight.

Lord Berners, British composer, writer and artist, on
T. E. Lawrence – Lawrence of Arabia

Army: a body of men assembled to rectify the mistakes of the diplomats.

Josephus Daniels, US journalist

Violence is the last refuge of the incompetent.

Isaac Asimov, US author

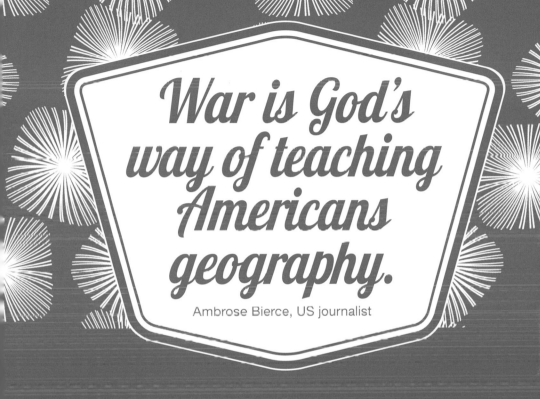

War is God's way of teaching Americans geography.

Ambrose Bierce, US journalist

Military justice is to justice what military music is to music.

Groucho Marx, US comedian

War is too important to be left to generals.

Georges Clemenceau, French Prime Minister

Force always attracts men of low morality.

Albert Einstein, German physicist

Men make war to get attention. All killing is an expression of self-hate.

Alice Walker, US author

A lamentably successful cross between a fox and a hog.

James G. Blaine, US politician, on US soldier Benjamin Franklin Butler

It is not the business of generals to shoot one another.

British soldier and statesman Arthur Wellesley, Duke of Wellington

Gentlemen, when the enemy is committed to a mistake, we must not interrupt him too soon.

Horatio Nelson, British admiral and national hero

May God have mercy for my enemies because I won't.

George S. Patton, US General

Nearly a quarter of American men were in the Armed Forces. The rest were in school, in prison, or were George W. Bush.

Bill Bryson, US author

One must not judge everyone in the world by his qualities as a soldier: otherwise we should have no civilization.

Erwin Rommel, German Field Marshal

Military Mockery

Everyone wants peace - and they will fight the most terrible war to get it.

Miles Kington, British journalist

War is only a cowardly escape from the problems of peace.

Thomas Mann, German writer

A prisoner of war is a man who tries to kill you and fails, and then asks you not to kill him.

Winston Churchill, British Prime Minister

It is forbidden to kill; therefore all murderers are punished unless they kill in large numbers and to the sound of trumpets.

Voltaire, French writer

Military Mockery

I tell you Wellington is a bad general, the English are bad soldiers ... we will settle this matter by lunch time.

Napoleon Bonaparte, French dictator, before the Battle of Waterloo

Waterloo was a battle of the first rank won by a captain of the second.

Victor Hugo, French writer, on British general the Duke of Wellington

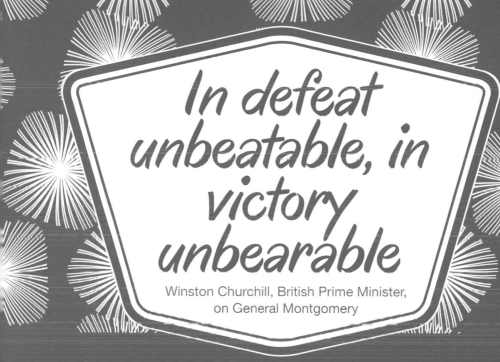

*In defeat
unbeatable, in
victory
unbearable*

Winston Churchill, British Prime Minister,
on General Montgomery

*At the age of four with paper hats and
wooden swords we're all generals. Only
some of us never grow out of it.*

Peter Ustinov, English actor

The General is suffering from mental saddle sores.

Harold L. Ickes, US Politician, on
General Hugh S. Johnson

If my soldiers were to begin to think, not one of them would remain in the army.

Holy Roman Emperor Frederick II

Why does the Air Force need expensive new bombers? Have the people we've been bombing over the years been complaining?

George Wallace, US politician

It will be a great day when our schools have all the money they need, and our air force has to have a bake-sale to buy a bomber.

Robert Fulghum, US author

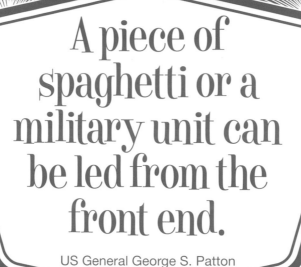

A piece of spaghetti or a military unit can be led from the front end.

US General George S. Patton

The British soldier can stand up to anything except the British War Office.

George Bernard Shaw, Irish playwright

Don't say it's impossible! Turn your command over to the next officer. If he can't do it, I'll find someone who can, even if I have to take him from the ranks!

General Thomas 'Stonewall' Jackson, US soldier

A soldier will fight long and hard for a bit of coloured ribbon.

Napoleon Bonaparte, French dictator

Military Mockery

REAR, noun:
In American military matters, that exposed part of the army that is nearest to Congress.

Ambrose Bierce, US journalist

I am not fond of speaking about politics because I don't have in my possession an army of 200,000 soldiers.

Franz Liszt, Hungarian composer

I sort of sympathize with them looking for weapons of mass destruction, because I'm like that with scissors. Honestly, I just turn the house upside down. Of course the difference is I know I have *got* some scissors.

Linda Smith, British comedian, on 'the Iraq crisis'

Military Mockery

I guess if you're stupid enough to join the army without thinking about getting shot at, then you really are a fool.

James Blunt, British singer-songwriter and former soldier

My hope is that gays will be running the world, because then there would be no war. Just a greater emphasis on military apparel.

Roseanne Barr, US comedian

The only time he ever put up a fight in his life was when we asked him for his resignation.

Georges Clemenceau, French Prime Minister, on French general, Jean-Jacques Joffre

The Army has carried the American ideal to its logical conclusion. Not only do they prohibit discrimination on the grounds of race, creed and color, but also on ability.

Tom Lehrer, US musician

A nation that continues year after year to spend more money on military defence than on programmes of social uplift is approaching spiritual death.

Martin Luther King, Jr., US civil rights activist

Standing at the head of his troops, his drawn salary in his hand.

Henry Labouchère, English politician and publisher, on the Duke of Cambridge

You really can't blame the military for wanting to go to war [in Iraq]. They've got all these new toys and they want to know whether they work or not.

Andy Rooney, US TV and film writer

Military men are the scourges of the world.

Guy de Maupassant, French writer

No good decision was ever made in a swivel chair.

US General George S. Patton

War and drink are the two things man is never too poor to buy.

William Faulkner, US writer

MacArthur is the type of man who thinks that when he gets to heaven, God will step down from the great white throne and bow him into His vacated seat.

Harold L. Ickes, US politician, on General Douglas MacArthur

I have just read your dispatch about sore-tongued and fatigued horses. Will you pardon me for asking what the horses of your army have done since the battle of Antietam that fatigues anything?

Abraham Lincoln, US President, replying to a dispatch from General McClellan, complaining about the condition of the Union cavalry

Aim towards enemy.

Instructions on US rocket launcher

He who joyfully marches to music rank and file has already earned my contempt. He as been given a large brain by mistake, since for him the spinal cord would surely suffice.

Albert Einstein, German physicist

Military Mockery

I would rather have a German division in front of me than a French one behind me.

US General George S. Patton

President Bush is trying to put a positive spin on the latest bad economic numbers. Today he declared victory in the 'War on Jobs'.

Craig Kilborn, US chat show host

One of the revolving lighthouses which radiate momentary gleams of light and then suddenly relapse into complete darkness. There are no intermediate stages.

David Lloyd George, British Prime Minister, on British Field Marshal Lord Kitchener

Our army is composed of the scum of the earth - the mere scum of the earth.

British General, The Duke of Wellington

The Canadian military is like Switzerland's. Without the knife.

John Wing, Canadian comedian and author

The number of medals on an officer's breast varies in inverse proportion to the square of the distance of his duties from the front line.

Charles Edward Montague, British journalist

We, the willing, led by the unknowing, are doing the impossible for the ungrateful.

Unattributed (on life in the army)

Never trust a man who combs his hair straight from his left armpit.

Alice Roosevelt Longworth, daughter of US President
Theodore Roosevelt, on General Douglas MacArthur

The nuclear arms race is like two sworn enemies standing waist deep in gasoline, one with three matches, the other with five.

Carl Sagan, US astronomer and author

I think I understand what military fame is: to be killed on the field of battle and have your name misspelled in the newspapers.

Union General William Tecumseh Sherman, during the American Civil War

Military Mockery

A mother discussing her son's military career with Abraham Lincoln:

Mr President, you must give me a colonel's commission for my son. Sir, I demand it, not as a favour, but as a right. My grandfather fought at Lexington. My uncle was the only man that did not run away at Bladensburg. My father fought at New Orleans, and my husband was killed at Monterey.

Abraham Lincoln:

I guess, madam, your family has done enough for the country. I think the time has come to give somebody else a chance.

The ever more sophisticated weapons piling up in the arsenals of the wealthiest and the mightiest can kill the illiterate, the ill, the poor and the hungry, but they cannot kill ignorance, illness, poverty or hunger.

Fidel Castro, Cuban Prime Minister

After the Duke of Wellington left me, I entirely forgot him: nay, before.

Harriet Wilson, English Regency courtesan

Wars are poor chisels for carving out peaceful tomorrows.

Martin Luther King, Jr., US civil rights leader

The mail service has been excellent out here, and in my opinion this is all that the Air Force has accomplished during the war.

Lewis B. 'Chesty' Puller, US general, in a letter to his wife from Korea

All war is a symptom of man's failure as a thinking animal.

John Steinbeck, US writer

Military Mockery

My dear McClellan, if you don't want to use the army, I should like to borrow it for a while.

Abraham Lincoln, US President, to General McClellan who had raised a powerful army, but seemed disinclined to seek battle

Older men declare war. But it is youth that must fight and die.

Herbert Hoover, US President

The military caste did not originate as a party of patriots, but as a party of bandits.

H. L. Mencken, US journalist

There is no flag large enough to cover the shame of killing innocent people.

Howard Zinn, US historian and writer

Military Mockery

The general is a stumpy, quadrangular little man, with a forehead of no promise and hair so short that it looks like a coat of black paint.

US Major General George Strong, on General Philip H. Sheridan

Take the diplomacy out of war and the thing would fall flat in a week.

Will Rogers, US actor

Heroism on command, senseless violence, and all the loathsome nonsense that goes by the name of patriotism - how passionately I hate them!

Albert Einstein, German physicist

I fired him because he wouldn't respect the authority of the President. I didn't fire him because he was a dumb son-of-a-bitch, although he was, but that's not against the law for generals. If it was, half to three-quarters of them would be in jail.

Harry Truman, US President, on General Douglas MacArthur

There are three kinds of intelligence - the intelligence of man, the intelligence of animals, and the intelligence of the military. In that order.

Gottfried Reinhardt, German film director

We are especially not going to tolerate these attacks from outlaw states run by the strangest collection of misfits, Looney Tunes and squalid criminals since the advent of the Third Reich.

Ronald Reagan, US President, after two Arab terrorists hijacked a TWA plane and landed it in Beirut

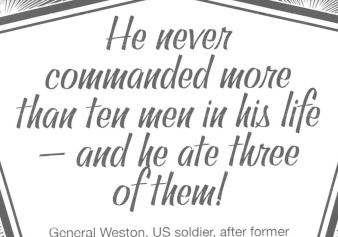

He never commanded more than ten men in his life — and he ate three of them!

General Weston, US soldier, after former Arctic explorer Adolphus W. Greely was made a general

How can you have a war on terrorism when war itself is terrorism?

Howard Zinn, US historian and writer

Military Mockery

From some traits of his character which have lately come to my knowledge, he seems to have been so hackneyed in villainy, and so lost to all sense of honour and shame that while his facilities will enable him to continue his sordid pursuits there will be no time for remorse.

George Washington, US President, on traitor Benedict Arnold

Even if a submarine should work by a miracle, it will never be used. No country in this world would ever use such a vicious and petty form of warfare!

William Henderson, British admiral, 1914

Madam, I have seen their backs before.

British general, The Duke of Wellington, when the French marshals, smarting from their defeat at Waterloo, turned their backs on him at the Vienna Conference

The signs of the Vietnam War protestors said, 'Make Love not War!' It didn't seem to me that they were capable of either.

Ronald Reagan, US President

As far as Saddam Hussein being a great military strategist, he is neither a strategist, nor is he schooled in the operational art, nor is he a tactician, nor is he a general, nor is he a soldier. Other than that he's a great military man.

US General Stormin' Norman Schwarzkopf

Before a war military science seems a real science, like astronomy; but after a war it seems more like astrology.

Rebecca West, British author and journalist

I feel that retired generals should never miss an opportunity to remain silent concerning matters for which they are no longer responsible.

US General Stormin' Norman Schwarzkopf

The direct use of force is such a poor solution to any problem, it is generally employed only by small children and large nations.

David Friedman, US scholar

Men are basically smart or dumb and lazy or ambitious. The dumb and ambitious ones are dangerous and I get rid of them. The dumb and lazy ones I give mundane duties. The smart ambitious ones I put on my staff. The smart and lazy ones I make my commanders.

German Field Marshal Erwin Rommel on his selection methods for staff

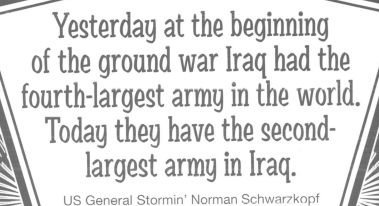

Yesterday at the beginning of the ground war Iraq had the fourth-largest army in the world. Today they have the second-largest army in Iraq.

US General Stormin' Norman Schwarzkopf speaking at a news conference during Operation Desert Storm

I hate nobody except Hitler — and that is professional.

Winston Churchill, British Prime Minister

Military Mockery

The professional military mind is by necessity an inferior and unimaginative mind; no man of high intellectual quality would willingly imprison his gifts in such a calling.

H. G. Wells, English writer, on soldiers

If Hitler invaded Hell I would make at least a favourable reference to the Devil in the House of Commons.

Winston Churchill, British Prime Minister

Going to war without France is like going deer hunting without your accordion.

US General Stormin' Norman Schwarzkopf

Military Mockery

Glory is fleeting, but obscurity is forever.

Napoleon Bonaparte, French dictator

When I lost my rifle, the Army charged me 85 dollars. That is why in the Navy the Captain goes down with the ship.

Dick Gregory, US comedian

As far as I'm concerned, war always means failure.

French President Jacques Chirac

As far as France is concerned, you're right.

Rush Limbaugh, US talk show host, replying to Chirac

It is only those who have neither fired a shot nor heard the shrieks and groans of the wounded who cry aloud for blood, more vengeance, more desolation. War is hell.

William Tecumseh Sherman, Union General and writer

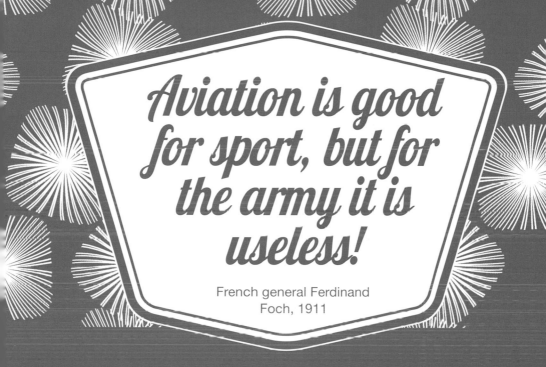

Aviation is good for sport, but for the army it is useless!

French general Ferdinand Foch, 1911

Our bombs are smarter than the average high school student. At least they can find Kuwait.

A. Whitney Brown, US writer and comedian

The old lie: dulce et decorum est pro patria mori.

Wilfred Owen, English war poet

Classic
Put-downs

Sporting
Slam Dunks

Sporting Slam Dunks

Running a marathon is no great hardship compared to the tortuous ordeal of being interviewed afterwards.

Sally Gunnell, British athlete

Golf is a good walk spoiled.

Mark Twain, US writer

Golf is played by twenty million mature American men whose wives think they are out having fun.

Jim Bishop, US journalist

The natural state of the football fan is bitter disappointment, no matter what the score.

Nick Hornby, English author

Sporting Slam Dunks

He's never going to be a great player on grass. The only time he comes to the net is to shake your hand.

Goran Ivaniševic, Croatian tennis player, on Ivan Lendl

New Yorkers love it when you spill your guts out there. Spill your guts at Wimbledon and they make you stop and clean it up.

Jimmy Connors, US tennis player

You can't see as well as these flowers and they're plastic!

US tennis player John McEnroe to a line judge

I'm not having points taken off me by an incompetent old fool. You're the pits of the world.

US tennis player John McEnroe to umpire Edward James

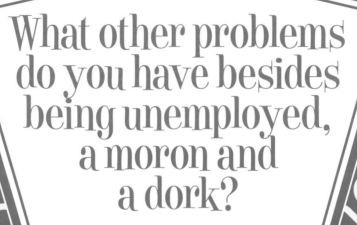

What other problems do you have besides being unemployed, a moron and a dork?

US tennis player John McEnroe
to a heckling spectator

All hockey players are bilingual.
They know English and profanity.

Gordie Howe, Canadian ice hockey player

I never questioned the integrity of an umpire. Their eyesight, yes.

Leo Durocher, US baseball player and manager

I never comment on referees and I'm not going to break the habit of a lifetime for that prat.

Ron Atkinson, English soccer coach

I've seen George Foreman shadow boxing ... and the shadow won!

Muhammad Ali, US boxer

Why waltz with a guy for 10 rounds if you can knock him out in one?

Rocky Marciano, US boxer

I'll beat him so bad he'll need a shoehorn to put his hat on.

US boxer Muhammad Ali ahead of a fight
against Floyd Patterson

English Boxing abolitionist Baroness Edith Summerskill
to boxer Henry Cooper:

Mr Cooper, have you looked in the mirror lately and seen the state of your nose?

Cooper:

Well, madam, have you looked in the mirror and seen the state of your nose? Boxing is my excuse. What's yours?

Me and Jake LaMotta grew up in the same neighbourhood. You wanna know how popular LaMotta was? When we played hide and seek, no one looked for him.

Rocky Graziano, US boxer, on his long-time rival

He makes the Elephant Man look like Pamela Anderson.

English boxer David Haye on rival Nikolai Valuev

Show me a good loser and I'll show you a loser.

Vince Lombardi, legendary US
football coach

His pace is deceptive; he's slower than you think.

Bill Shankly, Scottish soccer coach, about England captain
Bobby Moore

Tell them that I totally disagree with whatever it is they're saying.

Bill Shankly, Scottish soccer coach, when surrounded by a group of journalists talking Italian

Dracula is more comfortable with crosses.

Mike Maguire, UK radio host and prankster, interviewing England soccer coach Sven-Göran Eriksson on the subject of goalkeeper David James

Football is a fertility festival. Eleven sperm trying to get into the egg. I feel sorry for the goalkeeper.

Bjork, Icelandic musician, with her unique view of soccer

Pele should go back to the museum.

Diego Maradona, Argentinian soccer player, responds to criticism from the Brazilian legend

That's so when I forget how to spell my name, I can still find my clothes.

Stu Grimson, Chicago Blackhawks' left wing, explaining why he keeps a colour photo of himself above his locker

Why'd your parents name you Stu, didn't they know how to spell stupid?

Grimson once again, on being put down over his lack of brain power

His limitations are limitless.

Danny Ozark, US baseball coach, on former player Mike Anderson

I can't really remember the names of the clubs that we went to.

US basketball legend Shaquille O'Neal on whether he had visited the Parthenon during his trip to Greece

The kid is the greatest proof of reincarnation. Nobody could be that stupid in one lifetime.

Joe McCarthy, US Major League Baseball Manager

We'll explain the appeal of curling to you if you explain the appeal of the National Rifle Association to us.

Andy Barrie, Canadian radio personality

Most people are using two-piece cues now, but Alex doesn't have one because they don't come with instructions.

Steve Davis, snooker player, on Alex 'Hurricane' Higgins

Like an octopus falling out of a tree.

David Feherty, Irish golfer, passes comment on Jim Furyk's swing

If a lot of people gripped a knife and fork the way they do a golf club, they'd starve to death.

Sam Snead, US golfer

My wife just had a baby.

US boxer Ken Norton

Congratulations! Whose baby is it?

US boxer Joe Frazier

Why would anyone expect him to come out smarter? He went to prison for three years, not Princeton.

US boxing promoter Dan Duva on Mike Tyson

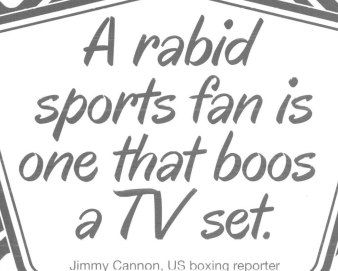

A rabid sports fan is one that boos a TV set.

Jimmy Cannon, US boxing reporter

I hate all sports as rabidly as a person who likes sports hates common sense.

H. L. Mencken, US journalist

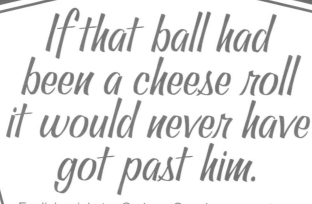

If that ball had been a cheese roll it would never have got past him.

English cricketer Graham Gooch comments on Mike Gatting's dismissal by Australian bowler Shane Warne as well as on his appetite

It couldn't have been Gatt. Anything he takes up to his room after nine o'clock, he eats.

Sir Ian Botham, England cricketer, defending teammate Mike Gatting from accusations of inappropriate behaviour with a barmaid

Australian cricketer Mark Waugh (twin of Steve) to England bowler Jimmy Ormond:

You're not good enough to play for England.

Ormond:

But at least I'm the best player in my family.

When in Rome, dear boy.

Cricketer Mike Atherton in response to being called a cheat by Ian Healy on England's tour of Australia

I'm not the next Anna Kournikova – I want to win my matches.

Maria Sharapova, Russian tennis player

If they can make penicillin out of mouldy bread, they can sure make something out of you.

US boxer Muhammad Ali to a young boxer

Joe Frazier is so ugly he should donate his face to the US Bureau of Wildlife.

Muhammad Ali, US boxer

Oi, Tufnell, can I borrow your brain? I'm building an idiot.

Australian spectator heckling English cricketer Phil Tufnell

Leave our flies alone, Jardine, they're the only friends you've got here.

An Australian spectator at Sydney upbraids the English cricket captain for swatting the local wildlife during the Bodyline series, perhaps the most hostile encounter ever between the cricketing arch-enemies

They say that nobody is perfect. Then they tell you practice makes perfect. I wish they'd make up their minds.

Wilt Chamberlain, US basketball player

Alan Shearer, he's boring, isn't he? We call him Mary Poppins.

Freddy Shepherd, Chairman of Newcastle FC, on his star player

If a man watches three football games in a row, he should be declared legally dead.

Erma Bombeck, US writer and humorist

[American] football combines the two worst features of American life: violence punctuated by committee meetings.

US journalist George Will sums up the US national game

Which one of you suckers is coming in second?

US basket ball player Larry Bird on entering the locker room before winning the first Basketball All Star 3 Point shooting contest

You know it's going to hell when the best rapper out there is white and the best golfer is black.

Charles Barkley, US basketball player

Sporting Slam Dunks

He cannot kick with his left foot, he cannot head a ball, he cannot tackle and he doesn't score many goals. Apart from that, he's all right.

George Best, legendary Northern Irish soccer player, on David Beckham

Just when you thought there were no surprises left in football, Vinnie Jones turns out to be an international player.

Jimmy Greaves, English soccer legend, is shocked when hardman Jones is selected for Wales

I wouldn't be worried if we lost every game as long as we won the League.

Mark Viduka, Australian soccer player

Football is all right as a game for rough girls but is hardly suitable for delicate boys.

Irish writer Oscar Wilde makes a fair comment on soccer – years before anyone started to dive to win free kicks

Sporting Slam Dunks

Golf appeals to the idiot in us and the child. Just how childlike golf players become is proven by their frequent inability to count past five.

John Updike, US writer

Golf is a day spent in a round of strenuous idleness.

William Wordsworth, English poet

This is my island, my culture. Don't you be staring at me. In my culture we just bowl.

West Indian cricket captain Viv Richards to Australian fast bowler Merv Hughes

In my culture we say get lost!

Hughes' response

He has everything a boxer needs except speed, stamina, a punch, and the ability to take punishment. In other words, he owns a pair of shorts.

US columnist Blackie Sherrod on a heavyweight boxing contender

He has turned defensive boxing into a poetic art. Trouble is, nobody ever knocked anybody out with a poem.

Eddie Shaw, US boxing coach, about Herol Bomber Graham

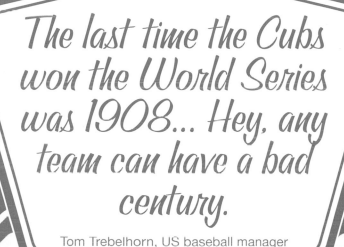

The last time the Cubs won the World Series was 1908... Hey, any team can have a bad century.

Tom Trebelhorn, US baseball manager

What's the difference between a 3-week-old puppy and a sportswriter? In six weeks, the puppy stops whining.

Mike Ditka, US NFL player, coach and commentator

At eight o'clock I settle into my armchair to watch an England game on TV. An hour and a half later, I look at my watch and it says a quarter past eight.

Jimmy Greaves, English soccer legend, on England under Sven-Göran Eriksson

I don't think heading a ball has got anything to do with it, footballers are just stupid anyway.

An English Premier League spokesman comments on a report that brain cells are damaged by heading soccer balls

What Carew does with a football, I can do with an orange.

Swedish soccer player Zlatan Ibrahimovic on compatriot John Carew

Showing off is the fool's idea of glory.

Bruce Lee, US actor and kung fu specialist

They finally found it.

A self-deprecating Eddie 'the Eagle' Edwards on being asked how his brain was following a brain scan after a ski-jumping accident

It's red, round and weighs about five ounces, in case you were wondering.

Greg Thomas, Welsh cricketer, unwisely makes fun of Viv Richards' inability to hit the ball. Richards soon smashes it out of the ground and replies:

Greg, you know what it looks like. Now go and find it.

Sporting Slam Dunks

The bad news for Saddam Hussein is that he's just been sentenced to the death penalty. The good news for Saddam is that David Beckham is taking it.

Anonymous reflection on David Beckham's penalty kicking ability

Football players, like prostitutes, are in the business of ruining their bodies for the pleasure of strangers.

Merle Kessler, performance artist

He hits from both sides of the plate. He's amphibious.

Yogi Berra, US baseball legend

Baseball has the great advantage over cricket of being sooner ended.

George Bernard Shaw, Irish playwright

Football is not just a matter of life and death; it's much more important than that.

Bill Shankly, Scottish soccer coach

College football is a sport that bears the same relation to education that bullfighting does to agriculture.

Elbert Hubbard, US journalist

Lie down so I can recognize you.

Willie Pep, US featherweight boxer, when asked by an old opponent if he remembered him

Serious sport has nothing to do with fair play. It is bound up with hatred, jealousy, boastfulness, disregard of all rules and sadistic pleasure in witnessing violence. In other words, it is war minus the shooting.

George Orwell, English author

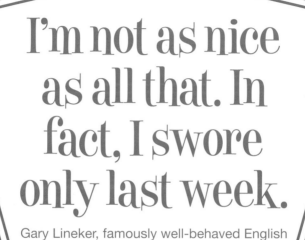

I'm not as nice as all that. In fact, I swore only last week.

Gary Lineker, famously well-behaved English soccer player

He's got more previous than Jack the Ripper.

Harry Redknapp, English soccer coach, on striker John Hartson, renowned for his physical approach

You can make a lot of money in this game. Just ask my ex-wives.

Lee Trevino, American-Mexican golfer

I don't want to play golf. When I hit a ball, I want someone else to go chase it.

Rogers Hornsby, US baseball player

Mr Agnew, I believe you have a slight swing in your flaw.

Jimmy Demaret, US golfer, to his playing partner, US Vice-president Spiro T. Agnew

You can all throw your medals in the bin because they were not won fairly.

Soccer coach Brian Clough alienates the Leeds United stars at his first training session as manager

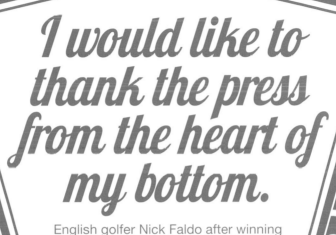

I would like to thank the press from the heart of my bottom.

English golfer Nick Faldo after winning the 1992 Open

I was showing early symptoms of becoming a professional baseball man. I was lying to the press.

Roger Kahn, US author

Only if there's an outbreak of bubonic plague.

Giovanni Trapattoni, Italian soccer coach, when asked if Paolo Di Canio would be selected

SUPERCALIGOBALLISTIC CELTICAREATROCIOUS

Mary Poppins-style headline in the *Sun* newspaper after Celtic FC were beaten in the third round of the Scottish Cup by lowly Inverness Caledonian Thistle in 2000

80 per cent of the top 100 women are fat pigs who don't deserve equal pay.

Dutch tennis player Richard Krajicek, the 1996 Wimbledon champion

What I meant to say was that only 75 per cent are fat pigs.

Later clarification by Krajicek

Roseanne Barr is a bowling ball looking for an alley.

Mr Blackwell, US fashion critic

303

Sporting Slam Dunks

Sharks are as tough as those football fans who take their shirts off during games in Chicago in January, only more intelligent.

Dave Barry, US writer

If you don't calm down, you'll live up to your name.

England prop Gareth Chilcott to Welsh prop Dai Young

Nice job. Now go and have another donut, fat boy.

An old ice hockey put-down, reportedly used by players congratulating an official on a job well done.

Many baseball fans look upon an umpire as a sort of necessary evil to the luxury of baseball, like the odour that follows an automobile.

Christy Mathewson, US baseball player

My missus could have scored that!

Harry Redknapp, English soccer coach, when his centre-forward Darren Bent headed past an open goal

I was always a sports nut but I've lost interest now in whether one bunch of mercenaries in north London is going to beat another bunch of mercenaries from west London.

John Cleese, British actor, on the money in English soccer

You've got to remember that under that cold professional Germanic exterior beats a heart of stone.

English racing driver Damon Hill, Formula One world champion, on Michael Schumacher

The man who views the world at 50 the same as he did at 20 has wasted 30 years of his life.

Muhammad Ali, US boxer

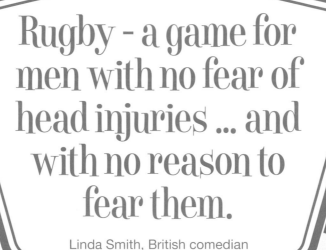

Rugby - a game for men with no fear of head injuries ... and with no reason to fear them.

Linda Smith, British comedian

I went to a fight the other night, and a hockey game broke out.

Rodney Dangerfield, US comedian

She's so stupid she returns bowling balls because they've got holes in them.

US comedian Joan Rivers on actress Bo Derek

She can't be with us tonight. She's busy attending the birth of her next husband.

English snooker player John Parrott on Joan Collins

I never said most of the things I said.

Yogi Berra, US baseball legend

There was a vacancy when I left, and the owners decided to continue with it.

Albert 'Happy' Chandler, on being replaced by Ford Frick as US Baseball Commissioner

Is that your real face or are you still celebrating Halloween?

Sir Ian Botham, English cricketer, to Rodney Marsh, Australian cricketer

Rugby is a good occasion for keeping thirty bullies far from the centre of the city.

Oscar Wilde, Irish writer

Players lose you games, not tactics. There's so much crap talked about tactics by people who barely know how to win at dominoes.

Brian Clough, English soccer coach

Ally MacLeod thinks tactics are a new kind of mint.

Scottish comedian Billy Connolly on Scotland's soccer coach

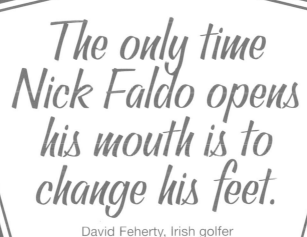

The only time Nick Faldo opens his mouth is to change his feet.

David Feherty, Irish golfer

I need a doctor immediately. Ring the nearest golf course.

Groucho Marx, US comedian

I know why he's bought a house by the sea - so that he'll be able to go for a walk on the water.

Fred Trueman, English cricketer, on Geoff Boycott, over-confident Yorkshireman and cricketer

I wouldn't say I was the best manager in the business. But I was in the top one.

Brian Clough, English soccer coach

For years I thought the club's name was Partick Thistle nil.

Scottish comedian Billy Connolly on one of the less successful Glasgow teams

We're a team in transition. We're going from bad to worse.

Kevin Keegan, English soccer coach, on his team Newcastle United

A wee club in the North East.

Manchester United soccer coach Sir Alex Ferguson dismisses Newcastle United

Sporting Slam Dunks

I don't know if Kournikova will sue, but it would be the only court appearance she's ever likely to win.

US baseball player Ken Rudolph on the Russian tennis player and model Anna Kournikova

I'm not saying he's pale and thin, but the maid in our hotel room pulled back the sheets and remade the bed without realising he was still in it.

Brian Clough, English soccer coach, about his player Brian Rice

They say he's an intelligent man, right? Speaks five languages! I've got a 15-year-old trainee from the Ivory Coast who speaks five languages!

Sir Alex Ferguson, Manchester United soccer coach, on arch-rival Arsene Wenger, the professorial French coach of Arsenal

Sporting Slam Dunks

It's good that Mike Tyson's been granted parole. More enlightened steps like this should be taken to make our prisons safer places.

US sports writer Greg Cote, *Miami Herald*

People who live in glass jaws shouldn't throw punches. The biggest danger in fighting Bruno is that you might get hit by flying glass.

Jim Murray, US journalist, on British heavyweight Frank Bruno

Tell him he can have my title. But I want it back in the morning.

US boxer Jack Dempsey's response when a drunk
challenged him to a fight

Tommy Morrison proved that he is an ambidextrous boxer. He can get knocked out with either hand.

Mike Tyson, US boxer